SCORPIONS

ANIMALS WITHOUT BONES

Jason Cooper

Rourke Publications, Inc.
Vero Beach, Florida 32964

PHOTO CREDITS
© James P. Rowan: cover, pages 4, 7, 8, 13, 17; © Breck Kent: title page; © Alex Kerstitch: pages 12, 21; © Lynn M. Stone: pages 10, 15, 18

Library of Congress Cataloging-in-Publication Data
Cooper, Jason, 1942-
    Scorpions / by Jason Cooper.
        p.   cm. — (Animals without bones)
    Includes index.
    Summary: A simple introduction to the physical characteristics, life cycle, and habitat of some of the many species of scorpions.
    ISBN 0-86625-573-7
    1. Scorpions—Juvenile literature. [1. Scorpions.] I. Title.
II. Series: Cooper, Jason, 1942-   Animals without bones.
QL458.7.C66   1996
595.4'6—dc20   95-46038
                                                    CIP
                                                    AC

Printed in the USA

TABLE OF CONTENTS

SCORPIONS

Scorpions are little, boneless animals known for the stingers in their "tails."

A scorpion's tail is really the long, slender end of its body. A scorpion often carries that part of its body like a tail, curling high over its back.

Scorpions are cousins of spiders and tarantulas. They are also related to ticks, mites, and the big, hard-shelled horseshoe crabs of the seashore.

An Israeli gold scorpion carries its tail like a flagpole

WHAT SCORPIONS LOOK LIKE

A scorpion has six pairs of what look like jointed legs. The first pair of legs is a pair of little **pincers** (PIN sirz). A scorpion's pincers are like tiny pliers, and they pinch.

The second pair of legs are claws that can grab and crush **prey** (PRAY), the animals scorpions catch. The scorpion uses the last four pairs of legs for walking.

Most scorpions are black, brown, or yellowish. They are 1/2 inch to 8 inches long.

The African scorpion's pincers are like little crab claws

KINDS OF SCORPIONS

Scientists have found hundreds of **species** (SPEE sheez), or kinds, or scorpions. Scorpions live all through the world. Only about 20 species live in the United States and Canada.

Different kinds of scorpions are often named for their actions or shape. Whipscorpions, for example, have a long, whip-shaped "tail" at the end of their bodies. Windscorpions are "quick as the wind."

This whipscorpion carries a "whip" instead of a long tail

SCORPION FAMILY

Scorpions belong to a group of small animals called **arachnids** (uh RAK nidz). About half of the 70,000 known kinds of arachnids are spiders. Arachnids like ticks and mites are *really* tiny creatures.

Arachnids have just two main body parts. The second part is the larger part. It's called the **abdomen** (AB duh men), and it has four pairs of walking legs. Insects have three pairs of walking legs.

Arachnids, like this green lynx spider, are among the least liked of all animals

11

The giant African scorpion looks like a black lobster, a not-too-distant cousin

A sand scorpion is at home in the dry desert of New Mexico

WHERE SCORPIONS LIVE

Scorpions live in many parts of the world. Most scorpions live in warm places.

Scorpions like hot, dry **habitats** (HAB uh tats), or homes. The deserts of Arizona and Mexico are favorite scorpion habitats.

Many scorpions live in warm, humid, tropical countries, too. A few species live in very cold countries. Scorpions can be found in Alberta, Canada, the Alpine Mountains of Europe, and the Andes Mountains of South America.

Traveling at night, this scorpion is hunting in a Central American rain forest

BABY SCORPIONS

Female scorpions give birth to live babies. Baby scorpions look like tiny copies of their parents. Some baby scorpions ride piggyback on their mothers for more than two months.

A mother scorpion protects her young. After the young scorpions become too big to ride on her, they strike off on their own.

Babies of an African black scorpion hitch a ride on their mother's back

HOW SCORPIONS LIVE

Scorpions are **predators** (PRED uh torz), or hunters. Like many animal hunters, they are **nocturnal** (nahk TUR nul) — they hunt at night.

During the day, scorpions hide in cool, dark places. They crawl under rocks, logs, leaves, tree bark — and even shoes. When hiding, a scorpion curls its tail along its side.

Scientists have learned that some scorpions can survive for a year without food.

A tailless whipscorpion waits for prey on a mossy tree trunk in Costa Rica

PREDATOR AND PREY

For a little guy, the scorpion is a scary predator. Its stinger delivers a jolt of poison that can hurt or kill its prey.

A scorpion does not use its poison except to defend itself. Instead, a scorpion kills prey with its claws. It uses its small pincers like fingers to pick apart its meal — finger food.

Scorpions eat spiders, insects, and other small animals. Larger scorpions can kill small mice and lizards.

A hairy scorpion feeds on a butterfly in Arizona

SCORPIONS AND PEOPLE

Scorpions defend themselves with their claws and stingers. Anyone who steps on a scorpion or handles one carelessly can get a nasty cut or sting.

Scorpion stings are painful, but they don't often kill people. However, one species of scorpion found in Arizona and Mexico can deliver a fatal, or deadly, sting.

People who live in scorpion country learn to always wear shoes. They also learn to look inside their shoes before putting them on!

Glossary

abdomen (AB duh men) — an important body part of some animals; the long, large second body section of a scorpion

arachnid (uh RAK nid) — a group of small, boneless, eight-legged animals, including spiders, ticks, mites, scorpions, and others

habitat (HAB uh tat) — the special kind of area where an animal lives, such as the leafy floor of a *rain forest*

nocturnal (nahk TUR nul) — active at night

pincers (PIN sirz) — "legs" that an animal uses to grip things; they work like pliers

predator (PRED uh tor) — an animal that kills other animals for food

prey (PRAY) — an animal that is killed by another animal for food

species (SPEE sheez) — within a group of closely-related animals, one certain kind, such as a *grizzly* bear

INDEX